cats
up close

To Brian,

A little memento
of our fellow-feeling
for the friendship of
funny punners.

Pat

Dec 1997

cats
up close

Vicki Croke

A Tiny Folio™
ABBEVILLE PRESS • PUBLISHERS
New York • London • Paris

contents

introduction 7

cats for all seasons 19

cats in action 97

kittens and cat-napping 123

the well-traveled cat 159

the industrious cat 215

cats & company 237

celebrity cat fanciers 265

selected bibliography 282
photography credits 283

introduction

What do we see when we look at cats up close?

Jeweled eyes. Slender, sleek, strong bodies. Affectionate, trusting souls. Independence. Sophistication. A spirit both wise and wiseacre.

Whether the cat by our side is a long hair, short hair, tabby, or tortoiseshell, we experience the same reaction: enchantment. Mysterious and elegant, playful and tender, cats are the most beguiling creatures our species has brought in from the cold.

But throughout history, cats have been a conundrum for societies. Secretive or sweet? Solitary or sociable? Spiritual or sinister? Physically, cats have not changed very much at all, but our perceptions of them have.

Unlike the dog (how unlike the dog!), one of the earliest domesticated animals, cats came to us relatively late. But they have more than made up for lost time, quickly taking up position not just in our homes, but in our hearts.

And we have marauding rodents to thank.

It was the advent of agriculture, and with it stores of grain, that brought us our sophisticated and predatory pals, probably more than three thousand years ago. It is believed that the African wild cat was employed in ancient Egypt to dispatch the mice and rodents of the Nile Valley who were siphoning off harvested grain stored in silos.

The ancient Egyptians did not stand a chance once they had lived with these dazzling creatures: they were spellbound. The cats adored by the ancient Egyptians were very much the cats we adore today. Art from this time depicts the cat just the way we see it in our living rooms, although then there was perhaps a bit more pomp surrounding the celebration of things feline.

The Egyptians worshipped a cat goddess named Bastet. She rode a chariot drawn by other cats (most of us can imagine our own cats choosing others from the neighborhood to be harnessed—"that snooping little calico from Oak Street . . . the big burly Tom from the backyard . . ."). Bastet was a powerful goddess closely related to the sun god Re.

Cats roamed a stone temple built in her honor and devotees studied their behavior for signs and signals from the great goddess herself. (We can, again, identify with these ancient Egyptians when we study our own cat's behavior for signals—"the salmon supreme or turkey giblet tonight? Give me a sign!"). In life, cats were loved; in death, they were mourned. If the household cat died, everyone in the Egyptian family would shave off their eyebrows.

But being worshipped is not always what it's cracked up to be, particularly in the twentieth century. In the United States, fifty-five million pampered cats have homes, while millions of others, unwanted, are euthanized every year. In Egypt, though the cat was held sacred, thousands were sacrificed and mummified. In one great temple, about three hundred thousand of these cat mummies, accompanied by a sort of bag lunch—mummified mice—were discovered just before the turn of the century.

Over several centuries, Bastet became more popular and powerful, drawing hundreds of thousands of promiscuous pilgrims to festivals celebrated with drinking, feasting, and wild sexual orgies. This history, along with nocturnal wanderings, reflective retinas that cause their eyes to "glow" in the dark, and the cat's natural pride (read as haughtiness), may have led to a shift in public opinion. Cats experienced dark times in medieval Europe, where they were linked to sorcery and witchcraft, and persecuted for hundreds of years because of this association. Though anti-cat hysteria began as early as the tenth century, the last cat known to be executed for sorcery in England died in 1712. And though we now understand what great companionship and solace cats can bring to the elderly, this precious relationship was misunderstood and destroyed during the Middle Ages. An old, solitary woman who communed with cats was always suspected of sorcery.

Black cats were especially singled out during witch hunts, and the superstition surrounding them still exists. In the United States, a black cat crossing one's path is supposed to mean bad luck, but in England it portends the opposite—trouble passed by without touching you—and is good luck.

Throughout even the darkest times writers remained cats' allies, as both shared a love of solitude and quiet. For example, Trecento Italian poet Petrarch (who inscribed on his cat's grave marker, "I was the greatest passion, second only to Laura") and sixteenth-century French essayist Michel de Montaigne ("When I am playing with my cat, who knows whether she has more sport in dallying with me, than I have in gaming with her?") remained loyal. And this relationship has continued through countless generations. Cats have gracefully made the transition from quill to laptop computer. Keats, Tennyson, Hardy, Twain, Kipling, and Colette loved cats and wrote fondly about them. It will come as no surprise to anyone who has witnessed the breathtaking athleticism of common cats that ultra-macho writer Ernest Hemingway was a true cat lover.

And he is hardly alone. It is that sleek muscularity that attracts so many of us. Despite domestication, cats have changed relatively little. We do not see in them the marked physical differences between the wild and domesticated varieties that we do in other "beasts of burden" (just try applying that term to your cat).

More than any other domesticated species, our little Muffy and Lulu can survive on their own. The ball of fluff purring on your warm lap knows very well how to snag a meal from the great outdoors—whether in a meadow or the mean streets of Manhattan.

In those deep, gorgeous eyes of azure blue or emerald green or warm amber we can glimpse the wild. With acute night vision, hearing tuned in to high-pitched sound, and a sense of smell thirty times better than our own, cats are built for predation. Whether country- or city-bound, cats who are allowed outdoors establish territories. They use scent to mark boundaries and employ brawn to enforce them (though threats usually do the trick).

Even the tiniest kittens are born with hunting instructions included. They have natural predatory instincts and hone their skills through play with their littermates. If you've seen them bat and bite, you know they are practicing for scrumptious, live mice. By watching a parent, they learn patience, pouncing technique, and how to deliver the predatory bite to the neck. The hunting instinct is strong; lacking a mouse, toes under a blanket, slippers slapping the floor, or a trailing shoelace will do.

Some domesticated cats hear the call of the wild. They revert to nature and are able to feed themselves with captured birds and rodents. They often reproduce prolifically, but tend to live to only half the age of a pampered house cat. In many cities, welfare groups work to sterilize and immunize stable feral cat populations.

And there is great controversy about whether cats should be allowed outdoors at all. Most animal protection groups say that cats should be kept indoors at all times, citing statistics that show how drastically life expectancy is reduced the moment a cat pads outdoors.

The age-old question for the owner is, "What makes my cat happy?" We know they are sensitive to touch, and they react with their entire bodies to our caresses. They shiver with delight and pass their heads and backs and rumps under our palms. Many cats find ecstasy in catnip—rolling and rubbing in it with wild abandon.

Their pleasures seem to come from simple things. A sun-drenched pocket of the room. A paper bag. The feel of their claws in upholstery. Marathon naps. Respect— all right, worship—from others.

Cats are curious and complex. Loving but independent. Domesticated but wild. Aloof and attentive. Felines are so many things that the only way to really catalog their stories is through pictures. No matter which type of cat is shown or where the photo was taken, you will recognize your own cat—its universal feline essence—in each shot.

Through these images, **cats up close** celebrates all that is eternal in cats.

17

cats for all
seasons

Though they would rather we did not know this fact, cats are rather hardy creatures. They are able to meet the changing seasons with robust metabolisms and are shrewd about finding both warm places in the winter and cool spots in the summer.

Still, most of us know "the look" only too well. We open the door for the cat one snowy afternoon, and after taking one look at the snow outside she sullenly holds us responsible. Yet usually they head out anyway. And what a picture we see as they enter the outdoor realm.

Each season frames our beautiful cats in rich new colors. The lush greens of summer combined with bright sunlight makes eyes glow and coats glisten. The autumn leaves, the winter snows, and spring rains invite different moods and include shadings from other palettes.

Whatever the season, we know that cats adore warmth, whether it involves lying in pools of sunlight in summer or curling up by a fire in winter. It can even alarm cat owners to see their pets so close to such intense heat, but their noses and lips act as little thermometers, warning them to get up and move away if it really gets too hot.

On a cold winter night a cat can be more helpful to us than a hot water bottle.

For one thing we don't have to refill our cats, and their coverings are much softer. And hot water bottles don't purr.

Cats can be found throughout the world and can live comfortably from the steamy equator to the frigid subantarctic. Thick coats and quick wits keep feral cats warm in colder climes. In equatorial heat, cats have thinner coats and can rid themselves of excess heat through sweat glands in the feet.

But why get overheated? We know that cats are quite shrewd about this. They work very hard, as we all know, to avoid overheating altogether.

And what does working hard at staying cool mean, exactly? Well, of course it means plenty of naps and slow movements in summer. (Naps seem to cure all kinds of problems, whatever the season.) In the fall, the chill puts a snap into their step (but still, plenty of time for napping) and through winter many are content to curl up under the blankets with us. We lose them a bit in the spring once again, as birds and bugs and blossoms take their thoughts elsewhere.

Whatever the time of year, wherever we are, we know that a home is always a cozier place with a cat.

Drinking in the fall foliage. The feline tongue curls backward to form a ladle for drinking water.

In the summer grass: slinky, sleek, and alert,
some domestic cats let us take a walk on the wild side.

A window on the world of cats.

The belly
roll
display is
a friendly
and
trusting
greeting.

The wise cat stocks winter provisions.

Like finding a feline in a haystack.

The wild beauty of cats allows us to look into
the eyes of nature itself . . .

. . . when they allow us to look.

And when cats look into our eyes, what do they see?

Autumn
leaves
make a
playground
paradise.

To every season, turn, turn, turn.

I can see clearly now, the pane is gone.

The shadows
grow longer,
the days
grow shorter,
but cats remain
consistent.

Foliage is not of interest to everyone.

A sunny spot can take the chill out of a fall day.

In bright sunlight, you can see how truly perfect cats are.
Da Vinci said even the smallest cat is "a work of art."

A rolling kitten gathers no moss.

45

Even a rotting log becomes elegant when
serving as a perch for a Siamese.

Do you hear what I hear?

Wild life on the forest floor.

Profiles in furrage.

Above it all.

Let it snow.

Snowbound.

A lion in winter.

There's a little Siberian tiger in many a household cat . . .

. . . and a bit of jungle cat in many more.

It's a jungle out here—and I love it.

How does your garden grow?

A little green always cheers me up.

In the pink.

Flower power.

To a
cat, an
empty
tub is a
good
tub.

The lush life.

Splendor in the grass.

At his post.

Ready to pounce (if absolutely necessary).

Royal purple for a regal cat.

Kittens in a basket.

Summertime and the living is easy.

The summer vegetation can—almost—hide a white cat.

Of course, some cats want to stand out.

The lazy days of summer.

Plucked from
obscurity

Gateway
to happiness.

A sunny disposition.

Kitty gets blue.

Kittens' curiosity.

A cat bouquet.

Not exactly puppy love.

Cats love to be secretive—
it's crucial to hunting in the wild.

Long arm of
the lawn.

Surprise!

The lazy days of summer? Try exhausting.

Cute as a kitten.

Don't fence us in.

Taking stock of summer.

There's nothing like the beginning of bug season.

Taking in the landscape.

Patrolling the summer grass, kittens can rotate
their ears and listen for voles. A cat's hearing is
five times better than our own in the higher ranges.

Petted by the light.

Portrait of a lady. The Scottish fold is noted
for its sweet personality.

cats in action

One of the cat's most captivating traits is that it can make the transition from happy house cat to powerful predator in one graceful leap.

House cats around the world are capable of "going feral" with an effortless ease afforded no other domesticated species. We know the pretty puss propped up on velvet cushions is only steps away from becoming a little tiger out in the meadow. Cats don't just talk the talk, they also walk the walk. With few exceptions, our domesticated darlings harbor the soul of the wild. They have finely tuned senses of sight, hearing, and smell. They have the bodies of supreme athletes, and the instincts of skilled hunters.

While it appears that we have wrestled and bullied and trapped other animals into captivity, cats may have strolled in. But they often show us how easily they can stroll out.

Mice, voles, and birds beware! Our cats were designed to catch you.

Cats move through branches with startling agility. A complex inner ear helps establish balance and a rudder-like tail maintains it. Cats also have at their command a full arsenal of hunting moves. For catching mice there is a quick downward strike. For birds, an upward leap. And for fish there is a flip of the prey onto land. All of these gestures are used by kittens in play, which strengthens muscles and hones techniques.

But our cats do not have to ford streams and scale mountains for a brush with the wild. A ball of yarn or a shoelace can become wily prey that needs to be stalked and subdued. The best toys are light enough to move quickly when batted and soft enough to sink teeth into.

It seems our cats establish quirky patterns of play during kittenhood and often keep them long into adult years. Even our frumpy, dignified middle-aged cats will surprise us and engage in a youthful romp with a balled up piece of paper or a length of string from time to time. Many cats display "mad moments," when their napping ends quite suddenly and all the stored up energy fuels several minutes of crazy dashing around the apartment.

Though sometimes it can be quite

distressing, our cats are efficient predators. Our two species first met up because of the cat's amazing ability to kill rodents. Now, however, we are often perplexed when our little companions bring home even smaller "companions"—a mouse, or worse still, half a mouse. How exact records are kept is anyone's guess, but books that keep tallies of such things often cite the world's best mousers, cats who are alleged to have dispatched tens of thousands of mice. Many of us would prefer that our cats work at ridding our apartments of balls of yarn.

First, check to see if the coast is clear. Next, it's a
portal to a barn full of milk. . . .

Branching out.

Leaping a wide brook in a single bound.

Cat overboard!

How is it that going up was so easy?

I'd rather be sailing.

Some cats prefer their laces al dente.

Though watching a kitten play is very cute, owners should also know that this play is how kittens learn survival skills for fighting and hunting.

Despite thousands of years of domestication, the cat has stayed fairly true to the wild in anatomy and behavior.

Barking up the wrong tree.

Suspended in time.

Drunk from too much twine.

Some cats live life with one paw in the gutter.

Cats may sleep sixteen hours a day, so when they're awake, they are really awake.

Something to flip over.

Reflections of an active cat.

Climbing the ladder to success.

With some cats it is easy to see the connection
between domestic and wild felines.

The stripes and the instincts of a tiger.

kittens and
cat-napping

It has been calculated that when a cat reaches nine years old, he or she has been awake for only three of them.

That means six years of naps, sound sleeps, dozes, cat naps, and snoozes. Six years of nose twitches, paw flickers, and ear blinks. Six years of sunny spots and pillows and cushions. Six years of rest and relaxation. Not bad.

It sounds like a joke, but the three year figure

is derived from the fact that the average house cat sleeps at least sixteen hours a day, twice that of the person lugging in the kitty litter and giant bags of food.

Like other efficient predators, cats are built to nap between kills. And that can be a nice, long time. The experts have even broken catnapping down into two different categories — the light sleep (ten to thirty minutes), and the deep, solid slumber (not more than ten minutes) with its rapid eye movement and limb twitches.

Our feline companions (surprise, surprise) don't go in for long periods of sleep like we do. They scatter theirs throughout a twenty-four-hour period (that's so they can be fully awake at the time you are in your soundest sleep).

In kittenhood and then again in old age,

cats sleep more—up to eighty percent of the day. It's easy to see why kittens do that. Weighing about four ounces at birth, kittens double that in just the first week. Then there are two months of suckling and growing and eye openings and tooth eruptions. That's a lot work.

But it seems the work of cats is to sleep anyway. Part of what we enjoy in cats is the sense of peace we feel when we see a contented cat curled up or stretched out in blissful slumber. The body is limp and the attitude is relaxed. When a wary predator such as our cat is asleep, it means no harm is near. There is nothing to fear. We relax, too.

Do cats dream? Scientists say brain wave activity during their deep sleep is similar to our own in that stage, but we cannot really tell if cats experience dreams the way we do.

The only way we'll be sure is if our cats learn to talk. But then, do we really want them stumbling downstairs in the morning in their little cat pajamas and boring us at the breakfast table with half remembered dreams the way friends do? "I was running through the backyard, chasing a mouse, well, it wasn't really a mouse . . . ."

A sleeping cat tells us all is right with the world. It brings us peace and tranquillity. And once you have shared your life with a cat, a pool of warm sunlight splashed across the floor just looks empty without a sweet cat dozing in it.

Dreaming of the Milky Way?

Head games.

They take after their father.

All this nursing is exhausting.

Taking a nap on the wild side.

Big,
bigger,
biggest.

Are you out of your gourd?

Swept away.

How to get cleaner, brighter whites.

Under the boardwalk.

These shoes were made for napping
and that's just what I'll do . . . .

Not a creature was stirring.

Garden of the feline-Continis.

Now blanket coverage.

After a snooze, she's got the world on a string.

Cat's cradle.

It's not comfortable, but it will do.

The hidden life of cats.

Who needs a scratching post?

Dreamy eyes. A cat's eyes tell us a lot
about mood. When the eyes are open wide,
the cat is alert; when the eyes are half-closed,
the cat is relaxed and trusting.

Please, do not disturb.

Come on 'a my barn.

Singing the praises of sleep.

Black and white and fur all over.

Turn out the lights already!

I didn't do it, **she** did it.

Kiss me, Kitty.

Sometimes it is best to also let sleeping **cats** lie.

the well-traveled cat

It is hard to imagine as we struggle to get our cats into carriers or into cars that they have such a well-traveled heritage. "I couldn't survive a two-block ride in the station wagon," they yowl. "How cruel to wrench me from hearth and home!" they scream. And yet not so many generations ago, our cats were navigating the uncharted seas, enjoying the life of the salty vagabond.

As soon as ships were used for trade, there wasn't one at sea that could hold down the healthy on-board rat population without a few ocean-going tabbies. Sailors valued their high seas mousers for keeping their stores of food safe, or at least much safer. That could be a matter of life or death on long voyages. To the crew, cats were heroes. And to the cats, the journey must have seemed like a vacation cruise—life was a constant banquet with plentiful food ready and warm. Rats on a raft, what could be better?

Felines today may have given up their seafaring ways in large part, but as we travel we get to see cats in exotic surroundings. They really don't appear any different the world over. (So how is it that in Paris even a scruffy calico can seem so . . . soignée? Maybe it's in the accented "miaou.")

Wherever in the world we find them, cats always look singularly at home. Everything can look out of place, except the cat.

They have a way of saying, "Of course I'm here, right where I belong." And we believe them. What setting could make a well-cut diamond look bad? It's impossible. The entire world was made for our cats.

The country cat, so fit and robust, hunting the meadow, overseeing the work in the barn—that's perfection.

The city cat, so self-possessed and sleek. This cat enjoys the nightlife—the lights along the skyline, the sounds of jazz in the air. And by day, there is so much to watch in the streets below, so much gossip to collect. This seems awfully perfect, too.

And who could be better placed than the lucky cat close to the water. Whether by fresh or salt water, there will always be plenty of fish. The portrait of this cat is also just right.

What we do know is that many cats have difficulty traveling or moving beyond their primary stomping ground. Are they sensitive to magnetic forces? Or are they just loathe to surrender any hard-won coziness?

A cat can kayak without ever touching an oar.

Keep on truckin'.

Taking the high road. Rudyard Kipling wrote of
the independent nature of cats in "The Cat
That Walked by Himself."

I'm ready for my close-up, Mr. DeMew.

You'll never guess who I bumped into today. . . .

Narrow, yes, but it will do.

Looks like rain to me.

There's always so much to see.

A meow with a French accent. This potted
cat calls Nice, France home.

Any family resemblance? Like their wild and distant relatives, cats know how to take care of themselves.

Two heads
are better
than one.

Oh my . . . . sardine truck at six o'clock.

Feline cityscape.

A step up
on the
social ladder.

Uh-oh, here comes Rover and his gang.

Cats on a hot terra-cotta roof.

Cat in a hat.

The peace of a park bench.

Ah, village life.

Cats in the belfry.

A place to be seen.

The ladies who bench.

My sill is my castle.

Paint the town red.

A simple, garden-variety cat.

Bewitching, no?

Steppin' out.

Cafe society.

Chairman of the bored.

Cathedral cat.

Palatial digs.

Reflections of feline beauty.

Backseat driver.

Way backseat driver.

The bars keep dogs **out**. They do not
keep cats **in**, however.

I could leave anytime I wanted. But why?

Sentry cat.

The weather is beautiful, and so am I.

A fire escape playground.

Born to
be mild.

Please, no shoes.

Still-life with cat.

Two cats with the blues.

the industrious cat

Cats and work?

The two must seem antithetical to those of us acting as the humble servants to a feline. But believe it or not, cats had a big job to do when they first began their association with us. And since then we have been employing them in all kinds of places. Unlike dogs, who have been bred to hunt or herd or guard, our cats usually have one mission: kill rodents. This skill has made cats invaluable to Egyptian farmers, hungry sailors, and to book lovers and postal clerks alike.

Wherever we have been victimized by nibbling vermin, we have been saved by pouncing, predatory cats. Hard-working cats have kept valuable tomes safe in libraries around the world. For in a library the cat is the perfect solution to a nasty problem. They keep mice from destroying valuable manuscripts, and they do it **quietly**. For more than a century, cats have been keeping England's post offices (a place filled with food parcels and paper) from being overrun by vermin. Cats have even helped various war efforts by killing rats aboard battleships.

In the world of high-stakes horse racing, cats have more than proved their worth as stablemates. There are famous stories that date from the 1700s about great racers who were wildly attached to feline companions. The 1945 Kentucky Derby winner, Daunt, was supposed to have shared a great bond with a tom named Ginger.

But while we think of the work of cats as being so singular in focus, there is another job they've moved into with absolute feline ease: stress reduction. Out of the barn and into our homes, one of the biggest jobs for cats today is keeping us happy and healthy. It is known, for example, that pets can lower our blood pressure and help us recover faster from injury or illness.

It is the job of the cat in modern society to meet us at the door and invite a greeting session. To sit on our laps on lazy days and purr. To keep us honest by never being impressed by our professional accomplishments. And to give us the same look whether we've just woken up with a bad case of "bedhead" or if we've just dressed for an evening out. They are accomplished stable-mates and soul mates.

We find them around the world, in all kinds of situations, but whatever job our cats take on, and wherever they do it, they pull it off with style and élan.

A kitten with the write stuff.

Siamese motto: Buy low, sell high.

Whiskers Fresno Firecracker Ampersand Circe Bozo Madeline Duchess Checkers
Norman Godzilla Hercules Shortstuff Dandelion Tigger Cyrano Abner Cupcake
Fuzzy Face Sylvester Bandit Rosaline Zeus Inkspot Slate Nova Nougat Jason
Ebony Venus Jingles Pandora Twinkle Toes Elvis Carlyle Sugar Camille Utah
Mickey Emily Anthracite Solo Saturn Chocolate Monty Kumquat Eggnog Quark
Cinderella Valentine Corkscrew Fireworks Princess Bruno Aurora Microchip
Tornado Marcus Juliet Kni   t Margo Phoenix Fluffy Socks Freedom Scorpio
Pica Falstaff Rambo S   lf Pint Nemo Nimbus Samson Pearl Rocky Picnic
Rufus Sherlock Cleo   ilver Tina Summer Midnight Hyphen Precious
Karma Othell   copia Winston Lucky Friday Neko Felix
Sweetheart P   araract Bodoni Nigel Bastet Max Cottontail
Deputy Orson   w Harley Prancer Goblin Galahad Kiko Dawn
Merlin Bill   Spokes Francois Butch Slate Zelda King Professor
Orbit Satin   mmetry Foxy Lady Mitzy Cody Asia Zachary
Captain Anna   on Syrup Punky Rudolf July Senator Mary
Kaleidosc   e Candy Morrison Bonnie Piglet Pickles
Jake Velv   rts Faith Moe Jewel Fransisco Ace Fiend
Pee Wee Ba   uentas Fritz Voodoo Ohm Sigmund Harmony Karl
Spot Harmonica   George Sir Stomper Ruth Fisher Jones Romeo Babs
Muffin Casey Bobo Vincent Thomas Furball Ralph Doc Bugs Justice Como Chopper
Whiskers Fresno Firecracker Ampersand Circe Bozo Madeline Duchess Checkers
Norman Godzilla Hercules Shortstuff Dandelion Tigger Cyrano Abner Cupcake
Fuzzy Face Sylvester Bandit Rosaline Zeus Inkspot Slate Nova Nougat Jason
Ebony Venus Jingles Pandora Twinkle Toes Elvis Carlyle Sugar Camille Utah
Mickey Emily Anthracite Solo Saturn Chocolate Monty Kumquat Eggnog Quark
Cinderella Valentine Corkscrew Fireworks Princess Bruno Aurora Microchip
Tornado Marcus Juliet Knight Margo Phoenix Fluffy Socks Freedom Scorpio
Pica Falstaff Rambo Sandy Half Pint Nemo Nimbus Samson Pearl Rocky Picnic
Rufus Sherlock Cleopatra Quicksilver Tina Summer Midnight Hyphen Precious
Karma Othello Muff Lenora Hero Cornucopia Winston Lucky Friday Neko Felix

Reading between the lines.

222

The very definition of a cat. Throughout history, libraries have employed cats to keep valuable books safe from marauding mice.

Basking in the glow of the fall sun.

Preparing for Halloween.

How do you take the measure of a cat?

Do I have to spell it out for you?

227

Some cats give
their all for art.

Some prefer the honest labor of life in the country.

Others enjoy the rugged seafaring life.

231

Drumming
up business.

Drugstore catboy.

The good life.

cats & company

If cats could befriend such a strange species
as ours, why should we be surprised when we find
them cuddled up with dogs or rabbits or lambs?

For all their fabled aloofness, our cats turn
out to be quite warm and friendly. Selective,
yes, always selective, but that does not preclude
affection. And it makes it all the more meaningful
when they do choose to spend some precious
time with us.

Cats are able to give and receive what we
very well might call love with an array of unlikely
partners. That's not so complicated really. But the

trouble with us humans is that we don't always recognize friendly signals in cats. They're subtle, and we don't always do well with subtlety. We often need to be hit over the head with affection (if that's physically possible).

Cats do not bowl us over with attachment the way dogs do, jumping and nudging. But notice that our cats so often stay close to us in a quiet and low-key way. They notice where we're going and they magically show up in the same room. They always happen to be precisely in the area where we are. A dog will follow you noisily from room to room, but a cat will shadow you without tipping his . . . paw.

They are, in fact, signaling sociability, but we don't always get it. Other animals, however, seem to pick up on the signs. The scenes are unmistakable: dire enemies—the cat and dog—curled up together on a sofa in a long, drawn-out grooming session. They have no trouble translating each other's body language. When a Great Dane "grooms" a little cat with a big wet lap, it may seem a bit coarse to the cat, but she puts up with it. Patience, hardly every attributed to cats, really does exist in those feline souls.

How many of us have seen our cats have to contend with a new puppy in the house? They may not be happy about it, they may stay at higher elevations for a while, but eventually they seem to teach these large, bold, young things the rules of the household.

And out in the barn, chickens and roosters may kick up more curiosity than affection in cats, but cows and horses often get the full kitty love treatment. And if a cow wanted to repay some of that feline friendliness with a little milk? Well, that would be fine, too.

Whether snoozing with a schnauzer or purring in our laps or even staring down barnyard fowl, it's clear our "solitary" cats love company.

And they said it wouldn't work out.
Though cats and dogs are supposed to be bitter
enemies, many live in absolute tranquillity.

Don't call my mother a dog.

Not a whiff of conflict.

An uneasy peace.

Really, I just want to be friends, come on out.
Movement triggers an instinctive hunting response in cats.

246

Ah, my little chickadee.

Cats are renowned hunters, and one of their most
important weapons is patience.

It may not be sportsmanlike, but it is fishing.

He's not the kind of cat some girls think of as handsome, but he unlocked the door to my heart.

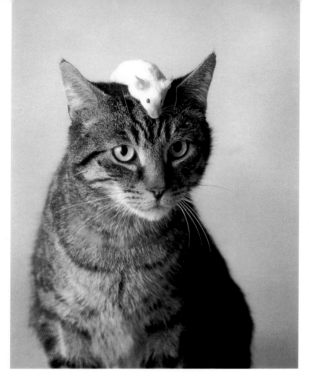

A different game of cat and mouse.

I know the milk is in there, I just don't know how to get it out. (Milk can actually upset the stomachs of many adult cats who are lactose intolerant.)

The cream of the crop.

Dearly beloved.

Anything can happen in the cabbage patch.

You are my sunshine.

Hand over an egg and no one gets hurt.

Love tap.

Evolutionary ladder?

Don't mess with my girls.

All creatures great and small.

Watch the birdie . . . .

celebrity
cat fanciers

Cats, probably more than any other domesticated animal, consider their owners both audience and caretaker. Every cat seems, very consciously at times, to be the star of his or her own feature film, complete with supporting cast (birds, mice), evil villain (the dog next door), exotic locales (window by front yard, window by back yard), red herrings (unused scratching post), and, occasionally, romance. And while many felines do seem to enjoy being gazed upon, they are also adept at summoning enough of a Garbo-esque, "I-vant-to-be-alone" act to keep the aching throngs (cat owners) at bay, and always wanting more.

So it may come as some surprise that these divas of home and hearth can in fact share the spotlight with a different breed of superstar, brightening movie screens around the globe with their stunning eyes and expressive faces alongside the great actors and actresses of the silver screen. As is often the way with a pretty face in Hollywood, the cats are usually typecast— as accomplice to Kim Novak's beautiful witch in **Bell, Book and Candle**; as pam-pered plaything for James Bond's nemesis Blofeld, or Brando's godfather—but they have also been given opportunities for branching out and exploring wider territory. Who could forget the pivotal, career-making roles played by cats in **Bringing Up Baby**, **Breakfast at Tiffany's**, and **Born Free**?

Off-screen, some cats have also made a career out of providing added glamour and sophistication to otherwise bland, posed publicity shots. Or, as is the case in this chapter's photograph of supermodel Cindy Crawford (page 279), of providing the requisite coverage to allow the enormous children's market safe access. After all, from **The Aristocats** and **Incredible Journey** to **The Lion King** and **That Darn Cat!**, cats both animated and live have been "me-wowing" youngsters for some time now.

Though it's easy to see why the famous seek out cats, it is perhaps less clear why cats would suffer the company of scene-stealing people. Perhaps it's a case of like attracting like. Or maybe it's just that cats have an uncanny knack for finding their way into pictures. As these photographs testify, cats do not pussyfoot around when it comes to milking a shot for all its worth.

Carole Lombard with her cat.

Elizabeth Taylor with one black beauty.

Kim Novak and her feline accomplice from **Bell, Book and Candle**.

Shirley Maclaine and friend.

Ernest Hemingway's trusted companion.

Vanna White, after stepping off the Wheel of Fortune, takes some time to comfort her kitty.

Linda Evans with another dynasty member.

Ivana Trump clearly knows all that glitters is not gold.

Cindy Crawford here models the new cat bra.
Watch those claws!

David Crosby with a new member of the band.

Even Davey Jones tires of monkeys.

selected bibliography

Cat Fanciers' Association Cat Encyclopedia.
New York: Simon & Schuster, 1993.

Caras, Roger. **A Cat Is Watching: A Look at the Way Cats See Us**. New York: Fireside, 1990.

Gebhardt, Richard H. **The Complete Cat Book.**
New York: Mirabel Books Ltd., 1991.

McHattie, Grace. **The Cat Lover's Dictionary.**
New York: Carroll & Graf Publishers, 1989.

Morris, Desmond. **Cat World: A Feline Encyclopedia.**
New York: Penguin, 1997.

Reader's Digest Illustrated Book of Cats. Pleasantville, N.Y.: Reader's Digest, 1992.

Siegal, Mordecai, ed. **The Cornell Book of Cats.**
New York: Villard Books, 1991.

Tabor, Roger. **Understanding Cats**. Pleasantville, N.Y.: Reader's Digest, 1995.

Thomas, Elizabeth Marshall. **The Tribe of the Tiger**.
New York: Simon & Schuster, 1994.

photography credits

The photographers and sources of photographic material
are as follows (numbers refer to pages):

Editor: Jeffrey Golick
Designer: Jordana Abrams
Picture Editor: Laura Straus
Production Manager: Stacy Rockwood

First edition
10 9 8 7 6 5 4 3 2 1

Library of Congress
Cataloging-in-Publication Data
Croke, Vicki.
    Cats up close / by Vicki Croke. — 1st ed.
        p.   cm.
    "A tiny folio."
    Includes bibliographical references
(p.   ).
    ISBN 0-7892-0198-4
    1. Cats. I. Title.
SF445.5.C74   1997
636.8—dc21   97-23691

selected list of tiny folios™ from abbeville press

- angels • 0-7892-0403-7 • $11.95
- ansel adams: the national park service photographs
  1-55859-817-0 • $11.95
- art of rock: posters from presley to punk
  1-55859-606-2 • $11.95
- barbie: in fashion • 0-7892-0404-5 • $11.95
- elvis: his life in pictures • 0-7892-0157-7 • $11.95
- the great book of french impressionism
  0-7892-0405-3 • $11.95
- hot rods and cool customs • 0-7892-0026-0 • $11.95
- the life of christ • 0-7892-0144-5 • $11.95
- minerals and gems from the american museum
  of natural history • 1-55859-273-3 • $11.95
- norman rockwell: 332 magazine covers
  1-55859-224-5 • $11.95
- treasures of folk art: the museum of
  american folk art • 0-7892-0409-6 • $11.95
- treasures of the louvre • 0-7892-0406-1 • $11.95
- wild flowers of america • 1-55859-564-3 • $11.95